ZOOMRIMES

Also by Sylvia Cassedy

Behind the Attic Wall
M. E. and Morton
Lucie Babbidge's House
Roomrimes

ZOOMRIMES
POEMS ABOUT THINGS THAT GO

Poems by Sylvia Cassedy · Pictures by Michele Chessare

HarperCollins*Publishers*

Zoomrimes
Poems About Things That Go
Text copyright © 1993 by the Estate of Sylvia Cassedy
Illustrations copyright © 1993 by Michele Chessare
All rights reserved. No part of this book may be used or reproduced
in any manner whatsoever without written permission except in
the case of brief quotations embodied in critical articles and reviews.
Printed in the United States of America. For information address
HarperCollins Children's Books, a division of HarperCollins
Publishers, 10 East 53rd Street, New York, NY 10022.
1   2   3   4   5   6   7   8   9   10
First Edition

Library of Congress Cataloging-in-Publication Data
Cassedy, Sylvia.
  Zoomrimes : poems about things that go / by Sylvia Cassedy ;
pictures by Michele Chessare.
      p.   cm.
  Summary: Twenty-six poems, all of which describe a means of
transportation or something that travels, ranging from "Ark" to
"Zeppelin."
  ISBN 0-06-022632-3. — ISBN 0-06-022633-1 (lib. bdg.)
  1. Children's poetry, American.   [1. Transportation—Poetry.
2. American poetry.]   I. Chessare, Michele, ill.   II. Title.
PS3553.A7953Z66   1993   90-1463
811'.54—dc20   CIP
                                                          AC

For David
S.C.

For my sisters, Pat and Noel,
with love and gratitude.
M.C.

CONTENTS

ZOOMRIMES

ARK

Packed
back to back
on rack after rack,
stacked nose to nose,
there they all are,
in series and rows,
all praying for drought.

And there's no going out:
All of them, *all*—

bug catchers
fly snatchers
chick hatchers
bone gnawers
flesh clawers
hole diggers
sap swiggers
chest puffers
down fluffers
wing strummers

foot drummers
tail thumpers
fence jumpers
earth heavers
web weavers
seed pluckers
blood suckers
vine braiders
stream waders
cud chewers
night mewers
day cooers
moon bayers
egg layers
hive dwellers
tree fellers
mud grubbers—
all of them,
ALL
forgot to bring rubbers.

BALLOON

Here, way up here,
in this box sort of thing,
slung in a tangle
of crisscrossed strings,
I dangle,
I hang.

Just over my head,
like a bubble of talk
in a joke-book cartoon,
is a giant balloon.

A moon
is embroidered in red
on its skin.
A hawk-nosed moon
whose single horn
meets, greets
a thorn-sharp chin.

Stars are there, too,
cross-stitched in blue,
and a sun:
a high-noon sun
with gold-spun cheek
and squint-eyed grin.

Moon, sun,
a streak of stars:
They are a message I send,
my bubble of talk,
to you,
to my friend far below,
as I go to the end of the sky.

And soon, clung
to a balloon of your own,
you reply:
"Mountain, field, sea,"
you say, in a bubble
of talk to me.
"Ocean, road, stone."

CAMEL

Tan
leather seats;
optional fur.
Sun roof. Runs on no gas. Stalls
seldom. Steers
with a whispered command to the ears.
Has four-leg drive. Hauls
anything: travelers, sleeping bags, frankincense, myrrh.
Overheats
never. An efficient sedan
is this passenger mammal.

DOGSLED

If someone should give me a dogsled
that was meant to carry *me*,
here's the first thing I would do with it:
Let all the dogs go free.
All, that is, but one,
and that I'd bundle up
in furs, and wraps,
and mitts, and caps
that covered all his head.
Then I'd settle him on pillows
in the middle of the sled,
and, crying out, "Let's go!"
I'd trundle him across the snow
of my backyard.

ESCALATOR

What if I miss?

What if,

instead of giving one great hop,

I squeeze,

flat as an envelope—

toes first,

knees next,

hair and fingers last of all—

through this slender slot?

What if, just where

this last stair

slopes into the swallow

of some dark space below,

I follow?

What would I see down there?

Another shop,

just like this,

but down side up?

FEET

For taking you places,
these
are the reasons
feet
are so great:

First, they're not late.
You don't have to freeze
at some platform or gate
for an hour or so,
when you're ready to go.
With feet,
you just *go*.

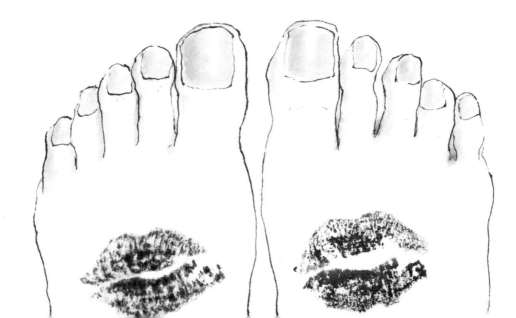

Also,
if *you* should be late,
they wait:
They don't slam their doors
in your face
when you've just given chase
down six floors
of your house
and through four city streets.
Feet wait.

What's more,
feet
are all yours.
You needn't compete
with ten other guys
for a space
or a seat
the size of a pea.

Besides,
feet are free.
No need to drop
lots of coins in a slot
just because you've decided
it's time for a ride.

In addition,
feet go where you say.
And *stay* where you say.
If, on your way,
you think you would
like to drop in on a shop,
they'll stop.

There's no scramble
for parking
with feet—
no need for stables,
garages, or barns.
They fit neatly
right under the table
and remain there,
barely
moving, while you eat.

So, why, if feet
are so great,
do I use them so rarely?

GALLEON

Here's where I stand:
in the blue-green sand
at the bottom
of my very own sea.

Among my masts
a shimmer of gold
swims in and out,
in and out,
like some restless ghost
returning, returning,
yearning for the chest
that had once been its home
in the foam-crusted dark
of my hold.

HELICOPTERS

One day each spring,
and I never know
which day it will be,
the tree outside my window
fills with a wind
all its own,
swells like a giant
silk parasol,
lets fall
a wondrous storm
of helicopters,
pale, pale green.

ICE SKATES

Two ball-point pens are what I have,
and one slick sheet of paper.
Now. Ready? Begin:
Roll some scrolls,
swing some rings,
twirl some curls,
loop some hoops,
whirl some swirls,
mark some arcs,
toe some bows,
reel some wheels,
twine some vines.
All done:
the largest,
the greatest,
the *coolest*
scribble-scrabble
ever.

JALOPY

Floppy, sloppy.
No top
has my jalopy.
Choppy, gloppy.
Drop
goes my jalopy.
Soppy, hoppy.
Clop
goes my jalopy.
Boppy, moppy.
Pop
goes my jalopy.
Loppy, ploppy.
Stop
goes my jalopy.
Stop
goes my jalopy.
Stop
goes my jalopy.
Stop.

KAYAK

A satisfying boat
is the kayak.
Each end the same:
its stem
no sharper than its stern.
No need for it to turn
around when heading home.
How very like its name
is this palindrome
afloat.

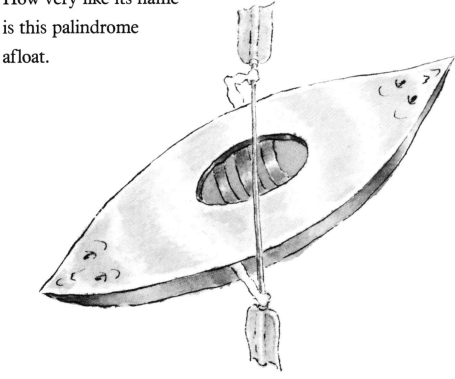

LIMO

Come now, every her and him-o, be you fat or be you slim-o; glad or grim-o; smart or dim-o; loud or prim-o; wide or trim-o; full of vig or full of vim-o. Cherubim and Seraphim-o, gather every life and limb-o; sing a psalm-o, sing a hymn-o, as you pile up to the brim-o, as you pile up to the rim-o, as you pile into my limo—lengthy, lissome, limber limo—pile into my new stretch limo.

MOON

Solitary
silver-white
sunlit wheel
blindly a-reel
on an unseen track,
where is the wagon
you left behind?
How many days till
it gets you back?

NIGHT TRAIN

Here comes the night train,
carrying night.
Stowed into packing crates,
corked into jars,
is a glimmer of light:
the glow of the moon,
the glisten of stars.

And listen!
Nailed into hampers,
bound into bales,
is a tumult of sound:
whoop of whippoorwill,
wail of loon,
whisper of vesper mouse,
scamper of rat,
wing-breath of bat,
whimper of cat.

And everywhere,
everywhere—
crowding the beams,
coating the door,
is a sauce of dark:
of soot,
of coal,
of crow-black bones,
of shadows peeled by day
from stones and walls,
of thunderclouds.

Here it comes,
the night train.
And here,
just as the sun drops
out of sight,
it stops,
slides wide
its doors,
spills out its freight,
filling everything,
everything—
fields, roads, holes, the sky—
with night.

OCEAN LINER

Now who could have had so crazy a notion—
to build a huge ship,
with bright polished things:
rings and rails and brass-capped nails;
and all kinds of spaces:
places for buying, for lying;
for swimming, for slimming;
for jogging, for jigging;
for running, for sunning;
for dining—
to build such a ship
and then use it for lining
the *ocean?*

PRAM

Pardon me, Ma'am,

but have you seen my pram?

The one with a slight spot of jam

at one end

and my Gram

at the other?

I'd meant just to

leave it a moment or two,

while my Gram

stopped to coo

at some dear little lamb

in another Gram's pram.

"Dear little lamb"

is just what she said,

patting its shoe

and the tam

on its head.

"You dear little lamb"

is just what she sighed,

while I slid down the side.

"For no more than a moment or two,"
I'd said, "though one will do," when Bam!
They were gone—my pram, my Gram.
Please, Ma'am, if you can't find my pram,
could you lend me five pence
for the tram?

QUEUE

The
life
of
this
queue
depends
only
on
you.
One
step
out
of
line

    and

    it

    all

    breaks

    in

    two.

ROCKING CHAIR

When Mama settles in the rocking chair,
she stretches herself out,
all thick and soft,
to make herself into a rocking chair lap,
so I can take
a rocking chair nap.

SUBWAY

Big snake
Slinks into view,
Rattles to a full stop,
Flourishes its wild painted skin.
Moves on.

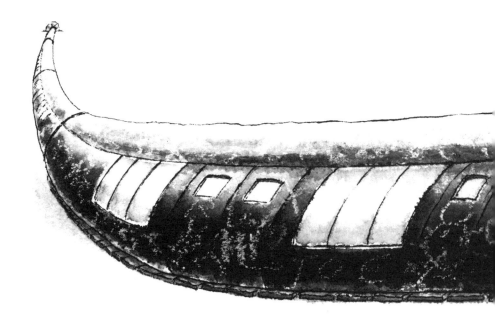

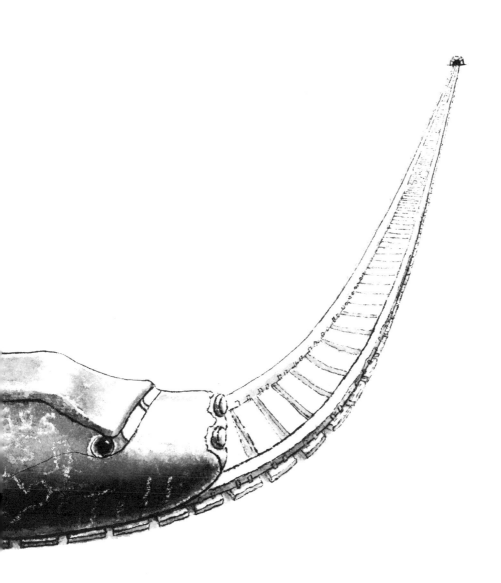

TOBOGGAN

Which is it, I wonder?
When they give me a push
at the top of the hill,
does the hill stay still,
or do I?
Do I fly
past
the trees,
the barn,
the frozen creek,
so fast
they are only a streak?
Or do they all fly
past me?

UNICYCLE

Who rides a unicycle?
A unicorn,
that's who:
a one-eared,
one-eyed,
one-nostriled
unicorn.
In a single-breasted
uniform.

VACUUM CLEANER

Like some greased beast
released
all at once
from its cave,
here comes the vacuum cleaner!

Slipping the lip
of its leathery trunk
high, low,
over, below,
it eats its lunch:

Munches on chunks of
jangling junk;
gulps down hunks of purple pulp;

Feeds on clumps of
seeds, of beads;
pecks at specks of
lint, of wool;

Picks at thick gray
wads of stuff:
dust,
hair,
spider fluff.

Crops, sips,
sucks, laps,
until, at last,
its belly full,
it backs itself
into its lair.

WHO AM I?

No chart have I,
no weatherglass,
no diagram of stars.
This way, that,

my course unknown,
I tack, drift,
shift, yaw,
swift as a bat,
bold as brass.

Nor do I sail alone:
Plucked from the sky,
a chaos of sea gulls—
gold of feather,
red of claw—
hangs close by;
darts at my decks, pecks
at the topmost tip
of my spars;
whirls, wheels,
reels, whips,
leaps
at my heel wherever
I go, swirls
to a heap
when I drop my sails,
finally sleeps.

X X X X X X

I sealed this note with kisses—
six in all—
each one a little cross of wings,
like vanes on a swinging windmill
or a wooden whirligig.
Then, as soon as they are posted,
just you wait and see!
The wings will all start spinning,
and fly my note to you
from me.

YACHT

When it's hacht, hacht, hacht,
and the sun's
like a fat squacht pacht
in the sky;
when a big clacht of sweat
makes a blacht in your eye
and you've gacht such a
knacht in your tum
from the heat
you would just as soon die,
here's whacht:
sail a yot.

ZEPPELIN

Zipper all the people in
the zeppelin
the zeppelin,
zipper all the people in
and let them sail away.